Neil Armstrong

Michael Collins

Edwin Aldrin

THE EAGLE HAS LANDED

THE EAGLE HAS LANDED

BY BILL MARTIN JR.
PAINTINGS BY FRANK ALOISE

Holt, Rinehart and Winston, Inc.
NEW YORK, TORONTO, LONDON, SYDNEY

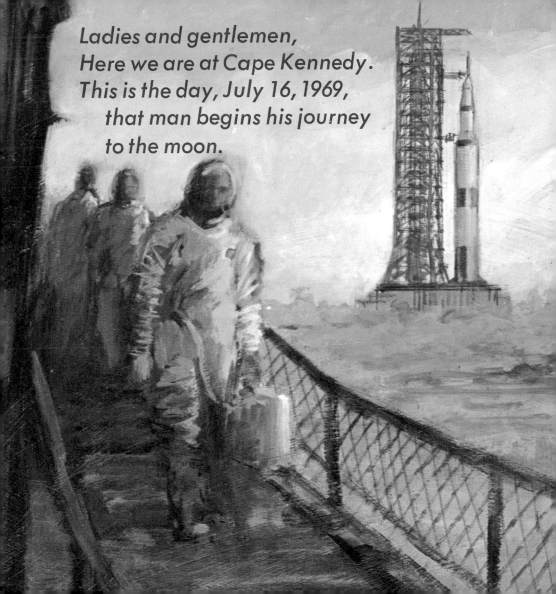

Ladies and gentlemen,
Here we are at Cape Kennedy.
This is the day, July 16, 1969,
  that man begins his journey
  to the moon.

10, 9, 8, ignition, 6, 5, 4, 3, 2, 1, 0.
All engines running.
Lift-off! We have a lift off!

We are now 2 minutes and 43 seconds into the flight.
Apollo 11 has reached an altitude of 217,655 feet,
    traveling at 6,141 miles per hour.
The first stage rocket has done its job!
Now it is jettisoned
    and the second stage rocket takes over.

9 minutes 11 seconds after lift-off!
Altitude 609,759 feet.
    15,468 miles per hour.
The third rocket engine takes over.
It's Go! for orbit around the earth!

2 hours, 44 minutes into the flight.
Apollo 11 lifts out of earth's orbit
at 24,182 miles per hour.
Man is on his way to the moon!

3 hours, 15 minutes into the flight. The astronauts release the moon-landing craft from its housing.

They dock the craft at the nose of the command ship
and continue the journey to the moon,
coasting through space.

July 19
75 hours and 50 minutes after lift-off.
A short burn of the rocket engine
    brakes the speed of Apollo 11
    and puts it into orbit around the moon.

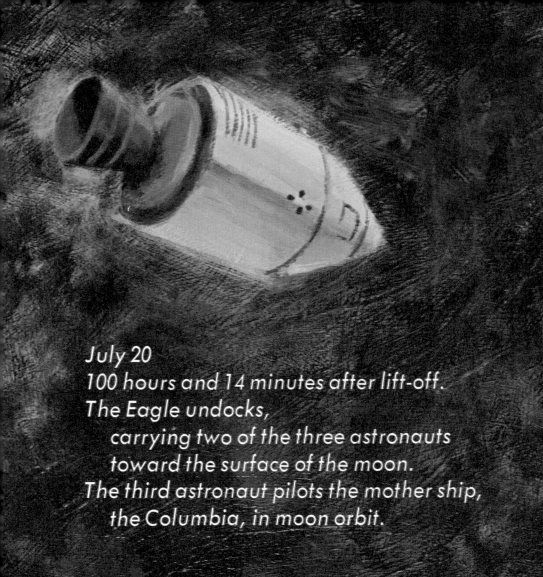

July 20
100 hours and 14 minutes after lift-off.
The Eagle undocks,
   carrying two of the three astronauts
   toward the surface of the moon.
The third astronaut pilots the mother ship,
   the Columbia, in moon orbit.

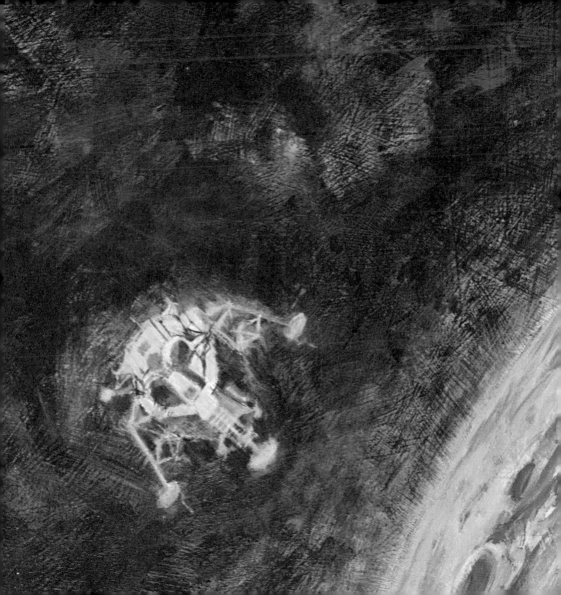

July 20, 1969
102 hours and 45 minutes into the flight.
''The Eagle has landed!''

July 21, 1969, 109 hours and 20 minutes into the flight.

Man walks on the moon!

124 hours and 21 minutes into the flight.
The Eagle rockets off of the moon
leaving its landing legs behind.

127 hours and 55 minutes into the flight.
The Eagle returns to the Columbia for docking.

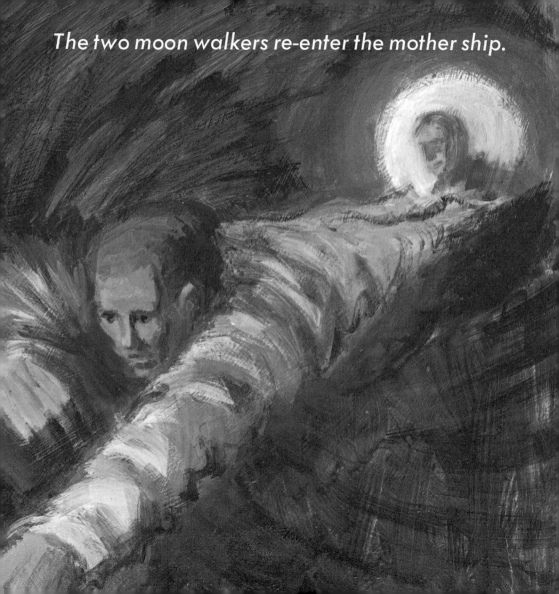
The two moon walkers re-enter the mother ship.

July 22
135 hours and 25 minutes into the flight.
Apollo 11 heads earthward,
    leaving the Eagle in aimless orbit
    around the moon.

July 24
Apollo 11 re-enters the earth's atmosphere,
    falling at 2,950 miles per hour,
    4,338 feet per second.
Now the astronauts jettison the third stage rocket.

194 hours and 50 minutes after lift-off.
The engineless ship, now a glowing capsule,
   falls toward the earth at 24,000 miles per hour,
   and heads for splashdown.

Splashdown!
The capsule is cradled in the Pacific Ocean.

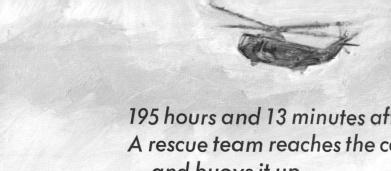

195 hours and 13 minutes after lift-off.
A rescue team reaches the capsule
and buoys it up.

The world's first moon-men are safely home.